EVERYDAY
Gratitude

INSPIRATION FOR LIVING LIFE AS A GIFT

Edited by
Saoirse McClory, Kristi Nelson, and Margaret Wakeley
A Network for Grateful Living

Storey Publishing

The mission of Storey Publishing is to serve our customers by
publishing practical information that encourages
personal independence in harmony with the environment.

EDITED BY Deborah Balmuth and
    Michal Lumsden
BOOK DESIGN AND LETTERING BY
    Alethea Morrison
WATERCOLORS AND COVER
    ILLUSTRATION © Katie Eberts,
    with additional watercolors by
    Clikchic Designs

See page 296 for source credits.

    The information in this book is true and
complete to the best of our knowledge. All rec-
ommendations are made without guarantee
on the part of the author or Storey Publishing.
The author and publisher disclaim any liability
in connection with the use of this information.

    Storey books are available for special
premium and promotional uses and for
customized editions. For further information,
please call 800-793-9396.

Storey Publishing
210 MASS MoCA Way
North Adams, MA 01247
storey.com

Printed in Hong Kong through Asia Pacific Offset
10 9 8 7 6 5 4 3

Library of Congress Cataloging-in-Publication Data

Names: A Network for Grateful Living.
Title: Everyday gratitude / by A Network for
    Grateful Living ; foreword by Brother David
    Steindl-Rast.
Description: North Adams, MA : Storey
    Publishing, [2018] | Includes bibliographical
    references.
Identifiers: LCCN 2017056547 (print) | LCCN
    2018010336 (ebook) | ISBN 9781635860474
    (ebook) | ISBN 9781635860634 (ebook) |
    ISBN 9781635860641 (ebook) | ISBN
    9781635860467 (paper with flaps and
    ribbon bookmark : alk.paper)
Subjects: LCSH: Gratitude–Quotations,
    maxims, etc. | Conduct of life–Quotations,
    maxims, etc.
Classification: LCC BJ1533.G8 (ebook) | LCC
    BJ1533.G8 E84 2018 (print) | DDC 179/.9–dc23
LC record available at https://lccn.loc.gov/
    2017056547

DEDICATED TO
THE TRANSFORMATIVE POWER
OF LIVING GRATEFULLY

FOREWORD
BY BROTHER DAVID STEINDL-RAST

_____

Many of us have heard Benjamin Franklin's advice: "Early to bed and early to rise, makes a man healthy, wealthy, and wise."

But, let's face it; no matter our gender, age, or most any other consideration, early rising does not enjoy widespread popularity, regardless of the promises attached to it. And for some of us *any* hour of rising seems early — too early. In more than 60 years of living by the monastic schedule, I ought to have gotten used to early rising. You would think so; but no! And I'm not the only one. One novice had already written and published a book about monastic life before he came to actually try living as a monk. The first morning after his arrival, when the excitator (a fancy name for the monk who wakes the others up) knocked on his door and called in Latin, *Benedicamus Domino!* ("Let us bless the Lord!") the novice was supposed to answer cheerfully, *Deo Gratias!* ("Thanks be to God!") Instead a muffled voice came from his bed: "This is a dog's life!"

The early bird may catch the worm, but most of us would prefer a more substantial breakfast, and definitely later. And yet, the way that blackbird leisurely hops through the dew-fresh grass when "morning has broken" stands in sharp contrast to the rush typical for most people's mornings. This is where *Everyday Gratitude* comes in, offering you a word of inspiration and a provocative question to start your day. "No! No!" I hear you shout: "I can't squeeze one more thing into the rush and scramble of my morning." But please, do give it a try! It takes less than a minute to read one of the quotes in this book and begin mulling over the accompanying question. That brief break may well transform your day.

This opportunity may even be worth making your alarm ring one minute earlier. And if you make it a habit to start the day with a passage from this delightful collection, grateful living *will* soon make you "sing praise for the morning." No matter how early or late you go to bed and rise, grateful living will make you healthy and wealthy and wise — healthy, through living in tune with the world; wealthy, because the grateful heart lacks nothing; and wise, because wisdom ripens as the most exquisite fruit in the garden of everyday gratitude.

Gut Aich Monastery, Austria
Summer 2017

INTRODUCTION

BY KRISTI NELSON

Executive Director, A Network for Grateful Living

"In daily life, we must see that it is not happiness that makes us grateful. It is gratefulness that makes us happy."

— BROTHER DAVID STEINDL-RAST

All of the world's great wisdom traditions teach us that life is precious and that what is happening right now *IS* life, not some future destination, time, or state of mind. "*Carpe diem,*" they say, implying that we must take none of this moment, and its opportunities, for granted. One way to do this is to live gratefully, with gratitude as the lens for our daily experiences. When we're able to do this, we notice what is already present, plenty, and abundant in our lives, from the tiniest things of beauty to the grandest of our blessings.

Even in the most challenging times, living gratefully makes us aware of, and available to, opportunities to learn and grow and to extend ourselves with care and compassion. We can see that life itself is a gift and that small, grateful acts every day can uplift us, make a difference for others, and help change the world. What we call gratefulness arises when we are connected to the "great-fullness" and privileges of our lives.

Approaching each day with a lens of gratitude, however, does not happen overnight. Gratefulness is nourished in small doses, through daily reminders, reflections, affirmations, and practices. It deepens with repetition and expands with support.

This book offers a collection of quotes, corresponding questions, and simple practices to uplift gratefulness and values such as compassion, kindness, interconnection, sufficiency, and love. Each quote, question, and practice also reflects at least one step on the path to grateful living:

1. STOP: *Pause and awaken.*

2. LOOK: *Become aware of the gifts and opportunities within and around you.*

3. GO: *Take action based on gratefulness and great-fullness.*

The point is not to become an expert in grateful living, never wavering from a grateful outlook. Rather, it is to recognize that gratefulness can offer each of us a touchstone to which we can return our awareness again and again. Gratefulness can make the ordinary things, moments, and people in our lives "pop" and become more extraordinary. It can help us see opportunities and gifts even in our difficulties. It can support us to marvel at things we have long taken for granted. And gratefulness is an important perspective-enhancer and can greatly improve quality of life for ourselves and others.

In short, gratefulness can make us happier. And who does not want to be happy?

In founding A Network for Grateful Living, Brother David Steindl-Rast created a global organization that inspires and guides individuals to act boldly with love, generosity, and respect toward one another, ourselves, and the Earth. We have been "preaching" and teaching gratitude since 2000, way before it was getting the public recognition it now enjoys. Members of our online community regularly tell us how our words of inspiration and questions for reflection make a meaningful difference in their days.

Turning toward reminders about what matters most deeply in life never grows old. It can stop us in our tracks and crack open our hearts, any time of day.

We hope you are drawn to this book for all of the promise it contains to enhance your happiness. We also hope that you are drawn to share this book with others for the same reasons. And ultimately, we hope that you will enjoy and share this book widely because we know that as more people live gratefully, together we can create a more loving, peaceful, thriving, and sustainable world — held as sacred by all.

May you find inspiration and meaning in these pages. May you become ever more grateful for the tremendous gifts of your life. And may you come to find happiness as a profound and steady companion.

Life is a gift. Every day is an opportunity — every moment a privilege. Thank you for making it matter.

WHEREVER YOU ARE IS THE ENTRY POINT

KABIR

What can I do right now, big or small, to help make a change I long for?

DO YOUR LITTLE BIT OF GOOD WHERE YOU ARE; IT'S THOSE LITTLE BITS OF GOOD PUT TOGETHER THAT OVERWHELM THE WORLD.

ARCHBISHOP DESMOND TUTU

When have I taken small steps with others to enact big change?

ALONE
WE CAN DO
SO LITTLE.
TOGETHER
WE CAN DO
SO MUCH.

HELEN KELLER

Have I expressed how helpful the people
in my life are to me?

WE LOSE TOUCH WITH OUR WINGSPAN WHEN WE HUNCH.

MARTIN SHAW

How am I being invited
to spread my wings right now?

People often say that
"beauty is in the eye of the beholder,"
and I say that the most liberating
thing about beauty is realizing that *you*
are the beholder. This empowers
us to find beauty in places where
others have not dared to look, including
inside ourselves.

SALMA HAYEK

What beauty can I find in this moment?

GRATITUDE PLACES YOU IN THE ENERGY FIELD OF PLENTITUDE. GLOW WITH GRATITUDE AND SEE HOW AWE AND JOY WILL MAKE THEIR HOME IN YOU.

MICHAEL BERNARD BECKWITH

How can I practice keeping the door open to awe and joy?

FOR ALL THAT HAS BEEN—
THANKS.
FOR ALL THAT SHALL BE—YES.

DAG HAMMARSKJÖLD

How might expressing gratitude today open me to grateful possibilities tomorrow?

WALLS TURNED SIDEWAYS ARE BRIDGES.

ANGELA DAVIS

How can I begin turning some of the
"walls" in my life into "bridges"?

GRIEF AND GRATITUDE ARE KINDRED SOULS, EACH POINTING TO THE BEAUTY OF WHAT IS TRANSIENT AND GIVEN TO US BY GRACE.

PATRICIA CAMPBELL CARLSON

Can I appreciate how each encounter today is unique, never to be repeated?

The more you sense the rareness and value of your own life, the more you realize that how you use it, how you manifest it, is all your responsibility. We face such a big task, so naturally we sit down for a while.

KOBUN CHINO OTOGAWA ROSHI

How can I honor all the wondrous events that took place so that I might be alive?

ONE KEY TO KNOWING JOY IS BEING EASILY PLEASED.

MARK NEPO

How has my being critical hijacked the possibility of joy?

SHOULD YOU SHIELD THE CANYONS FROM THE WINDSTORMS YOU WOULD NEVER SEE THE TRUE BEAUTY OF THEIR CARVINGS.

ELISABETH KÜBLER-ROSS

Who am I shielding?

Every wave on the ocean
is the whole ocean waving. . . .
So, the ocean of being waves every
one of us, and we are its waves.

ALAN WATTS

How do I understand or experience myself
to be a wave in the ocean?

EVERYTHING CAN BE
TAKEN... BUT ONE THING:
THE LAST OF THE
HUMAN
FREEDOMS—
TO CHOOSE ONE'S
ATTITUDE
IN ANY GIVEN
SET OF CIRCUMSTANCES,
TO CHOOSE ONE'S
OWN WAY.

VIKTOR E. FRANKL

What situation is beckoning me
to change my attitude?

IN ALL THINGS OF **NATURE** THERE IS SOMETHING OF THE **MARVELOUS.**

ARISTOTLE

What marvels are apparent to me in this moment?

✕

Seeing with Fresh Eyes

Walk through your kitchen or another room in your home as if you are seeing it for the first time. What do you notice with fresh eyes? What do you take for granted but might marvel at if you didn't? How does your home provide for you? Make a list of things you would find miraculous if you saw them anew.

Genius is the
ability to receive from
the Universe.

I CHING

What is the Universe offering me at
this moment?

LET US ACCEPT THE INVITATION, ever-open, FROM THE STILLNESS, TASTE ITS exQUISITE SWEETNESS, AND HEED ITS SILENT INSTRUCTION.

PAUL BRUNTON

When I pause to embrace the Stillness within,
what do I sense, what do I feel?

LET US
SLOW
DOWN
ENOUGH TO TRULY NOTICE ALL THAT IS PRESENTING ITSELF TO US AS BLESSING.

KRISTI NELSON

What gifts do I miss
when I am moving too quickly?

ATTENTION IS THE DOORWAY TO GRATITUDE, THE DOORWAY TO WONDER, THE DOORWAY TO RECIPROCITY.

ROBIN WALL KIMMERER

How can I cultivate my ability to pay attention?

Recipients of our appreciation are apt to express their own gratitude to others, lengthening the unending, golden chain of connections-in-goodness that stretches across the world.

MARY FORD-GRABOWSKY

How can I start a ripple of gratitude today?

THE LITTLE THINGS? THE LITTLE MOMENTS? THEY AREN'T LITTLE.

JON KABAT-ZINN

What little things and little moments matter to me?

GOODNESS OF HEART IS A CONTINUOUS FEAST.

PROVERBS 15:15

How am I fed by goodness of heart?

LET GRATITUDE
BE THE
PILLOW
UPON WHICH
YOU KNEEL
TO SAY YOUR
NIGHTLY PRAYER.

MAYA ANGELOU

Can I bow to the many ordinary and extraordinary
blessings that have enriched my day?

MAY YOU EMBRACE
THIS DAY, NOT JUST AS
ANY OLD DAY, BUT AS THIS DAY.
YOUR DAY.
HELD IN TRUST BY YOU,
IN A SINGULAR PLACE,
CALLED **NOW.**

CARRIE NEWCOMER

Is this moment the beginning of the rest of my
life or another reminder of the past?

Our drive to enlarge our *net* worth turns us away from discovering and deepening our *self*-worth.

LYNNE TWIST

What do I value? How might that benefit from my investment?

SURPRISE IS THE SEED OF GRATEFULNESS. BECOME AWARE OF SURPRISES. RELISH SURPRISE AS LIFE'S GIFT.

BROTHER DAVID STEINDL-RAST

What has surprised me lately?

FOR ME, LOSING... ISN'T FAILURE. IT'S RESEARCH.

BILLIE JEAN KING

What limiting beliefs do I wish to move beyond?

ALTHOUGH THE WORLD IS FULL OF SUFFERING, IT IS FULL ALSO OF THE OVER-COMING OF IT.

HELEN KELLER

Who has inspired me by overcoming adversity?

How many times have
you noticed it's the little quiet
moments in the midst of life
that seem to give the rest
extra-special meaning?

FRED ROGERS

What has been one of those
quiet moments for me?

WHEN THE BRIDGE IS GONE, THE NARROWEST PLANK BECOMES PRECIOUS.

HUNGARIAN PROVERB

When has the smallest gesture of kindness
made all the difference to me in going forward?

IT IS A **STRANGE** AND WONDERFUL FACT TO BE HERE, WALKING AROUND IN A BODY, TO HAVE A WHOLE WORLD WITHIN YOU AND A WORLD AT YOUR FINGERTIPS OUTSIDE YOU.

JOHN O'DONOHUE

What do magical events such as a phone call from someone I was thinking about teach me about my world?

TO BE ASTONISHED IS ONE OF THE SUREST WAYS OF NOT GROWING OLD TOO QUICKLY.

SIDONIE-GABRIELLE COLETTE

What has astonished me lately?

✕

Embracing Emotions

All feelings remind us that we are fully alive.
Challenging feelings connect us to our humanity,
and often, ironically, make us most lovable.
Like clouds, all emotions are temporary and
move through the sky of our life. Try holding
your emotions with compassion, wonder, and
gratitude.

I HAD NOT LOVED ENOUGH. I'D BEEN BUSY, BUSY, SO BUSY, PREPARING FOR LIFE, WHILE LIFE FLOATED BY ME, QUIET AND SWIFT AS A REGATTA.

LORENE CARY

What am I missing by keeping so busy?

NO ACT OF
KINDNESS,
NO MATTER HOW
SMALL,
IS EVER WASTED.

AESOP

What small kindness can I offer to others today?

GIVE
THANKS FOR
UNKNOWN
BLESSINGS
ALREADY ON
THEIR WAY.

NATIVE AMERICAN
PROVERB

Does following my intuition bring benefits
I could not have anticipated?

HAPPINESS IS NOT A MATTER OF INTENSITY BUT OF BALANCE AND ORDER AND RHYTHM AND HARMONY.

THOMAS MERTON

How can I bring more balance to my life?

When perfection exists as the nature of your Heart, why do you lose your composure by dwelling on imperfections?

SRI RAMANA MAHARSHI

How can I liberate myself from dwelling on imperfections?

HOW WONDERFUL WOULD IT BE, WHILE WE DISCOVER FARAWAY PLANETS, TO REDISCOVER THE NEEDS OF THE BROTHERS AND SISTERS ORBITING AROUND US.

POPE FRANCIS

What opens up when I attend with fresh eyes
and energy to the needs of those in my orbit?

NO ONE HAS EVER BECOME POOR BY GIVING.

ANNE FRANK

How have I been enriched by giving?

I BELIEVE THAT THE WORLD WAS CREATED AND APPROVED BY LOVE, THAT IT SUBSISTS, COHERES, AND ENDURES BY LOVE, AND THAT, INSOFAR AS IT IS REDEEMABLE, IT CAN BE REDEEMED ONLY BY LOVE.

WENDELL BERRY

What can those with whom I struggle
teach me about love?

WE ARE NEVER MORE THAN ONE GRATEFUL THOUGHT AWAY FROM PEACE OF HEART.

BROTHER DAVID STEINDL-RAST

How does gratitude make me feel whole?

To meet everything and everyone through stillness instead of mental noise is the greatest gift you can offer to the universe.

ECKHART TOLLE

What possibilities open when my mind is less busy and frenetic?

IT DOESN'T
TAKE MUCH —
IT CAN BE JUST
GIVING A
SMILE.
THE
WORLD
WOULD BE A MUCH
BETTER PLACE
IF EVERYONE
SMILED MORE.

SAINT MOTHER TERESA

What if I simply smile more often?

IN THE MIDST OF GATHERING DARKNESS, LIGHT BECOMES MORE EVIDENT.

BONNIE BOSTROM

What gives me hope in dark times?

Gratefulness allows us to nurture a keener eye that no longer rushes past the small everyday moments that make up the larger part of our lives.

GURI MEHTA

How can I nurture a keener eye?

THERE ARE HUNDREDS OF WAYS TO KNEEL AND KISS THE GROUND.

RUMI

How might my life change if I believed
that every moment is a gift?

HOW WE SPEND OUR DAYS IS, OF COURSE, HOW WE SPEND OUR LIVES.

ANNIE DILLARD

What habits can I shift so that the way I spend my days creates the life I want to live?

✕

The Treasure Chest

Reflect on memories of sweet moments in your life, large and small. Write each as a short line on a small piece of paper. Fold each memory and place it in a treasured container. Each day as you pass your "treasure chest," pull out and revisit a special memory.

My wish, indeed my continuing passion,
would be not to point the finger
in judgment but to part a curtain, that
invisible shadow that falls between
people, the veil of indifference to each
other's presence, each other's
wonder, each other's human plight.

EUDORA WELTY

To whose wonder or plight am I indifferent?

IT IS A POWERFUL PRACTICE TO BE GENEROUS WHEN YOU ARE THE ONE FEELING IN NEED.

ALLAN LOKOS

What happens when I act in service to others
when I am feeling down?

I RISE TO TASTE
THE DAWN,
AND FIND THAT
LOVE
ALONE
WILL SHINE
TODAY.

KEN WILBER

How can I help love shine today?

IF
WE *fall in love*
WITH CREATION
DEEPER AND
DEEPER,
WE WILL RESPOND TO
ITS ENDANGERMENT
WITH PASSION.

HILDEGARD OF BINGEN

What do I love so much that I would be
willing to make a great sacrifice for it?

STICKS IN A BUNDLE CANNOT BE BROKEN.

EAST AFRICAN PROVERB

Are there opportunities for me to join with others to make a difference?

When we trust our creativity we encounter a supreme kind of enjoyment — an amazement at the natural unfolding of life beyond our ordinary way of looking at things.

DZIGAR KONGTRUL RINPOCHE

What is revealed when I am creative?

GRATITUDE IS HAPPINESS DOUBLED BY WONDER

G. K. CHESTERTON

What moments fill me with wonder?

MAY YOU LIVE ALL THE DAYS OF YOUR LIFE.

JONATHAN SWIFT

Where in my life do I find playfulness and adventure?

When I dare to be powerful, to use my strength in the service of my vision, then it becomes less and less important whether I am afraid.

AUDRE LORDE

What can I bravely do today in service of something I am passionate about?

IF IN OUR DAILY LIFE WE CAN SMILE, IF WE CAN BE PEACEFUL AND HAPPY, NOT ONLY WE, BUT EVERYONE WILL PROFIT FROM IT. THIS IS THE MOST BASIC KIND OF PEACE WORK.

THICH NHAT HANH

How might my behavior change if I recognize my potential to spread peace in our world?

IF THE ONLY PRAYER YOU EVER SAY IN YOUR ENTIRE LIFE IS THANK YOU, IT WILL BE ENOUGH.

MEISTER ECKHART

How do I know when I have enough?

WHEN I STARTED COUNTING MY BLESSINGS, MY WHOLE LIFE TURNED AROUND.

WILLIE NELSON

What changes when I count my blessings?

THE ONLY WAY TO
MAKE SENSE OUT OF
CHANGE IS TO
PLUNGE INTO IT,
MOVE WITH IT,
AND JOIN THE
DANCE.

ALAN WATTS

Where in my life can I embrace change?

✕

Honoring Your Hands

Notice your hands and fingers, and think of the
strength, tenderness, and initiative they hold.
Think of all the extraordinary things they do for
you. Pause to offer them appreciation at various,
active moments throughout the day. Notice how
much they help to facilitate what you love in life.
Treat them gratefully.

There is within each of us a modulation, an inner exaltation, which lifts us above the buffetings with which events assail us. Likewise, it lifts us above dependence upon the gifts of events for our joy.

DR. ALBERT SCHWEITZER

How can I stay present in troubling times and, at the same time, access joy?

ATTENDING TO LIFE IS AN ACT OF LOVE.

KATIE RUBINSTEIN

What everyday chore can I look
at as an act of love?

GRATITUDE
IS THE
FAIREST
BLOSSOM
WHICH SPRINGS
FROM THE
SOUL.

HENRY WARD BEECHER

To whom can I offer a blossom
of gratitude today?

LIFE DOES NOT ACCOMMODATE YOU, IT SHATTERS YOU.... EVERY SEED DESTROYS ITS CONTAINER OR ELSE THERE WOULD BE NO FRUITION.

FLORIDA SCOTT-MAXWELL

How has being shattered allowed me to grow?

THANKS TO THE HUMAN HEART BY WHICH WE LIVE, THANKS TO ITS TENDERNESS, ITS JOYS, AND FEARS.

WILLIAM WORDSWORTH

How can I honor the tenderness within me?

HOW YOU DO ANYTHING IS HOW YOU DO EVERY-THING.

CHERI HUBER

What changes can I make to better align my choices with my deepest values?

Ultimately, we have just one moral duty: to reclaim large areas of peace in ourselves, more and more peace, and to reflect it towards others. And the more peace there is in us, the more peace there will also be in our troubled world.

ETTY HILLESUM

What would allow the reservoir of peace in me to overflow toward others?

HAPPINESS IS NOT WHAT MAKES US GRATEFUL. IT IS GRATEFULNESS THAT MAKES US HAPPY.

BROTHER DAVID STEINDL-RAST

When has being grateful made me happy?

THE BIG QUESTION
IS WHETHER YOU ARE GOING
TO BE ABLE TO
SAY A HEARTY
YES TO YOUR
ADVENTURE.

JOSEPH CAMPBELL

How can I live a big
YES to the adventure of my life?

We live in a time when science is validating what humans have known throughout the ages: that compassion is not a luxury; it is a necessity for our well-being, resilience, and survival.

ROSHI JOAN HALIFAX

To whom can I show compassion today?

THIS IS TRUE HUMILITY:
NOT THINKING LESS OF OURSELVES BUT THINKING OF OURSELVES LESS.

RICK WARREN

Who is an example of true humility?

JUST TO BE IS A BLESSING. JUST TO LIVE IS HOLY.

RABBI ABRAHAM JOSHUA HESCHEL

What is it I plan to do
with this one precious day?

I want to be famous in the way a pulley
is famous, or a buttonhole, not because it
did anything spectacular, but because it
never forgot what it could do.

NAOMI SHIHAB NYE

How can I appreciate my innate abilities?

WHEN YOU CAN DO THE COMMON THINGS OF LIFE IN AN UNCOMMON WAY, YOU WILL COMMAND THE ATTENTION OF THE WORLD.

GEORGE WASHINGTON CARVER

Which ordinary activities in my life might most benefit from an infusion of creativity?

ABUNDANCE IS NOT SOMETHING WE ACQUIRE. IT IS SOMETHING WE TUNE INTO.

WAYNE W. DYER

What is abundant in my life right now?

IT'S WISE TO
ACCEPT THAT
HUMAN FAULTS
ARE INEVITABLE.
FACTOR THAT IN AND
KEEP GOING.

ALICE WALKER

What changes when I don't expect perfection?

IN A WORLD
THAT LIVES LIKE A
FIST MERCY IS
NO MORE
THAN WAKING
WITH YOUR HANDS
OPEN.

MARK NEPO

Can I sense what might be possible if I loosen
my grip?

×

The Gifts of a Responsibility

Write down five things you feel you "have" to do in the course of your day or week, such as wash dishes, pay bills, or drive to work. Now, write those same things with the first three words, "I get to," and end with, "when so many people cannot." See how it feels to view your responsibilities as blessings or privileges.

Showing gratitude
is one of the simplest yet
most powerful things humans
can do for each other.

RANDY PAUSCH

To whom would it be meaningful to send
a handwritten letter or card?

WHEN WE ARE FULLY **ALERT** IN SPIRIT, MIND, AND BODY, WE ARE MORE THAN WE IMAGINE AND CAN ACCOMPLISH MORE THAN WE SUPPOSE.

BARBARA HOLMES

How can I become more awake in mind, body, and spirit?

every
ACT OF LOVE
IS A WORK OF PEACE
NO MATTER HOW
SMALL.

SAINT MOTHER TERESA

What small act of love can I offer today?

MAMA EXHORTED HER CHILDREN AT EVERY OPPORTUNITY TO "JUMP AT DE SUN." WE MIGHT NOT LAND ON THE SUN, BUT AT LEAST WE WOULD GET OFF THE GROUND.

ZORA NEALE HURSTON

When was the last time I took a leap of faith?

TO LIVE IS SO STARTLING, IT LEAVES BUT LITTLE ROOM FOR OTHER OCCUPATIONS.

EMILY DICKINSON

What worries get crowded out when
I awaken to the wonder of life?

Stepping out of the busyness, stopping our endless pursuit of getting somewhere else, is perhaps the most beautiful offering we can make to our spirit.

TARA BRACH

What if where I am and what I am doing right now is enough?

THE MYSTIC
IS NOT A SPECIAL HUMAN BEING— EVERY HUMAN BEING IS A SPECIAL KIND OF MYSTIC.

BROTHER DAVID STEINDL-RAST

How might I show up in the world
if I saw myself as a mystic?

AT THE HEIGHT OF *laughter,* THE UNIVERSE IS FLUNG INTO A KALEIDOSCOPE OF NEW POSSIBILITIES.

JEAN HOUSTON

What do I experience when I hear laughter?

EVERY INTERSECTION IN THE ROAD OF LIFE IS AN OPPORTUNITY TO MAKE A DECISION.

DUKE ELLINGTON

What hard decisions in my life can I
see instead as lucky choices?

"I AM GIFT." ALL THAT I AM IS SOMETHING THAT'S GIVEN, AND GIVEN FREELY. BEING DOESN'T COST ANYTHING. THERE'S NO PRICE TAG, NO STRINGS ATTACHED.

THOMAS MERTON

When I consider "I am gift," what feelings arise?

Too often we underestimate the power of a touch, a smile, a kind word, a listening ear, an honest compliment, or the smallest act of caring, all of which have the potential to turn a life around.

LEO F. BUSCAGLIA

Who needs my compassion right now?
How can I show it?

THAT'S WHAT I CONSIDER TRUE GENEROSITY: YOU GIVE YOUR ALL, AND YET YOU ALWAYS FEEL AS IF IT COSTS YOU NOTHING.

SIMONE DE BEAUVOIR

When have I given my "all"?

THE WORLD IS A PLACE WHERE THE EXTRAORDINARY CAN SIT JUST BESIDE THE ORDINARY WITH THE THINNEST OF BOUNDARIES.

JODI PICOULT

What wonders can I enjoy without spending a penny or going to exotic places?

MAKE VISIBLE WHAT, WITHOUT YOU, MIGHT PERHAPS NEVER HAVE BEEN SEEN.

ROBERT BRESSON

What is my unique contribution or expression?

Gratitude as a discipline involves a conscious choice. I can choose to be grateful even when my emotions and feelings are still steeped in hurt and resentment. It is amazing how many occasions present themselves in which I can choose gratitude instead of a complaint.

HENRI NOUWEN

What is a current situation in which I might choose gratitude instead of a complaint?

BEAUTY IS THE HARVEST OF PRESENCE.

DAVID WHYTE

When I listen with a quiet heart to a friend or stranger, what do I sense beyond their words, beyond their feelings?

✕

Kindness without Strings

Engage in an act of kindness. Notice if you are pulled toward kindness for a stranger or for someone close to you. Either way, offer your kindness with no strings attached and no need to be recognized. Truly. Notice the completeness of the act of giving, itself.

LOVE
DERAILS
WORLD-WEARY STRATEGY,
LOOSENS CYNICISM
FROM YOUR HEART,
LACES EVERY SINGLE
ONE OF YOUR BONES
WITH A COMPLETE
RE-BOOT OF WONDER.

MARTIN SHAW

What in my life might benefit if I let love do its thing?

OPPORTUNITIES, MANY TIMES, ARE SO **SMALL** THAT WE GLIMPSE THEM NOT AND YET THEY ARE OFTEN THE **SEEDS** OF GREAT ENTERPRISES.

OG MANDINO

What small opportunities have turned out to have made big differences in my life?

I have . . . learnt, from experience, that the greater part of our happiness or misery depends upon our dispositions, and not on our circumstances.

MARTHA WASHINGTON

Who do I know who is happy even in challenging situations? What can I learn from this?

WHEN YOU
DO THINGS FROM YOUR
SOUL,
THE RIVER ITSELF
MOVES
THROUGH YOU.
FRESHNESS AND A
DEEP
JOY ARE SIGNS
OF THE CURRENT.

RUMI

Where is the joy in this moment?

ACKNOWLEDGING THE GOOD THAT IS ALREADY IN YOUR LIFE IS THE FOUNDATION FOR ALL ABUNDANCE.

ECKHART TOLLE

Who are the beloved people and creatures that give my life a sense of abundance?

ONLY BY DEALING
WITH THE
DIFFICULTY
DOES THE
CREATIVITY
COME FORTH.

BRIAN SWIMME & THOMAS BERRY

What challenging situations have
brought out the best in me?

THE MORE THAT WE DEEPLY APPRECIATE, CARE FOR, AND FEEL INEXTRICABLY TIED TO THE PLACES, THINGS, AND PEOPLE OF THIS WORLD, THE MORE WE ARE LIKELY TO TAKE A STAND ON BEHALF OF WHAT WE VALUE.

KRISTI NELSON

How does fully opening my heart to what I value affect the choices I make?

The world is evolving from
imperfection to perfection. It needs
all love and sympathy;
great tenderness and watchfulness are
required from each one of us.

HAZRAT INAYAT KHAN

What or who needs my tenderness right now?

SOMETIMES OUR LIGHT GOES OUT, BUT IS BLOWN AGAIN INTO INSTANT FLAME BY AN ENCOUNTER WITH ANOTHER HUMAN BEING.

DR. ALBERT SCHWEITZER

Who has touched my life unexpectedly?

BE HAPPY

FOR THIS MOMENT. THIS MOMENT IS YOUR LIFE.

OMAR KHAYYAM

Can I be happy for this moment no matter the circumstances?

TO SPEAK GRATITUDE IS COURTEOUS AND PLEASANT, TO ENACT GRATITUDE IS GENEROUS AND NOBLE, BUT TO LIVE GRATITUDE IS TO TOUCH HEAVEN.

JOHANNES A. GAERTNER

How is living gratitude different from speaking it?

Wholeheartedness is a precious gift, but no one can actually give it to you. You have to find the path that has heart and then walk it impeccably. . . . It's like someone laughing in your ear, challenging you to figure out what to do when you don't know what to do. It humbles you. It opens your heart.

PEMA CHÖDRÖN

When have I let myself be led from an intuitive space in my heart?

BEING UNAPPRECIATIVE MIGHT MEAN WE ARE SIMPLY NOT PAYING ATTENTION.

DAVID WHYTE

What gifts are simply waiting for my attention?

THE THINGS THAT FRIGHTEN US JUST WANT TO BE HELD.

MARK NEPO

How might it feel if I gently held my fears
with compassion?

CALL OUT TO THE WHOLE DIVINE NIGHT FOR WHAT YOU LOVE. WHAT YOU STAND FOR. EARN YOUR NAME. BE KIND, AND WILD, AND DISCIPLINED, AND ABSOLUTELY GENEROUS.

MARTIN SHAW

What do I stand for?

Be the most ethical, the most responsible, the most authentic you can be with every breath you take, because you are cutting a path into tomorrow that others will follow.

KEN WILBER

How can I tend my path to make it clear and compelling to those who will follow?

WHEN we
COME UPON
BEAUTIFUL THINGS...
THEY ACT LIKE SMALL TEARS
IN THE SURFACE
OF THE WORLD THAT
PULL US THROUGH TO
SOME VASTER
SPACE.

ELAINE SCARRY

When have I experienced
being transported by beauty?

✕

Savoring a Meal

If you share a meal with others today, before or while you eat, ask each person to share something about the meal for which they are grateful. If you are eating alone, bring to mind something for which you are grateful and dedicate your meal to that "great-fullness."

EVERY TIME WE FEEL SATISFIED WITH WHAT WE HAVE, WE CAN BE COUNTED AS RICH, HOWEVER LITTLE WE MAY ACTUALLY POSSESS.

ALAIN DE BOTTON

How am I rich?

Gratitude for the gift of life is the primary wellspring of all religions, the hallmark of the mystic, the source of all true art.

JOANNA MACY & NORBERT GAHBLER

What does gratitude for the gift of life inspire in me?

We must learn to REAWAKEN and keep ourselves awake, not by mechanical aids, but by an infinite expectation of the DAWN.

HENRY DAVID THOREAU

How might I stay awake to all that is possible in this moment?

WEALTH CONSISTS NOT IN HAVING GREAT POSSESSIONS BUT IN HAVING FEW WANTS.

EPICTETUS

What are my wants versus my needs?
Can I release some of my wants?

REALITY IS PERMEATED, INDEED FLOODED, WITH DIVINE CREATIVITY, NOURISHMENT, AND CARE.

MARCUS J. BORG

So much goodness is available right now.
How am I missing it? How can I access it?

IF WE REALLY WANT TO BE **FULL** AND **GENEROUS** IN SPIRIT, WE HAVE NO CHOICE BUT TO **TRUST** AT SOME LEVEL.

RITA DOVE

Where do I hold myself back from being fully generous in spirit?